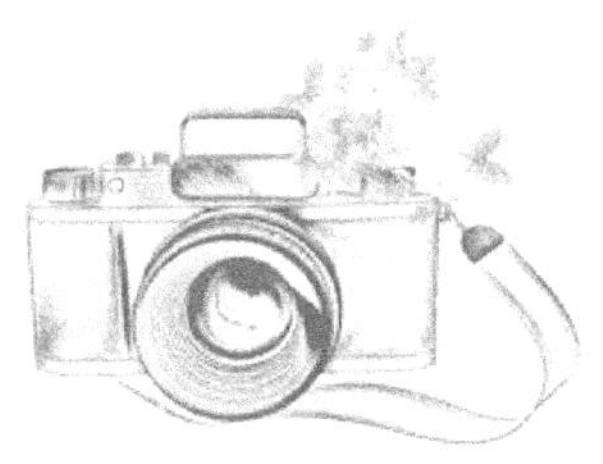

PHOTOGRAPHY LOG

This Book Belongs To:

____

____

____

Year At A Glance

JANUARY

FEBRUARY

MARCH

APRIL

MAY

JUNE

Year At A Glance

JULY	AUGUST	SEPTEMBER

OCTOBER	NOVEMBER	DECEMBER

Yearly Profit/Loss Report

YEAR	# ORDERS	INCOME	EXPENSE	PROFIT/LOSS

TOTALS:

Monthly Profit/Loss Report

MONTH	# ORDERS	INCOME	EXPENSE	PROFIT/LOSS
JAN				
FEB				
MAR				
APR				
MAY				
JUN				
JUL				
AUG				
SEP				
OCT				
NOV				
DEC				
TOTALS:				

Monthly Planner

MONTH OF:

MONDAY	TUESDAY	WEDNESDAY	THURSDAY

Monthly Planner

MONTH OF:

FRIDAY	SATURDAY	SUNDAY	NOTES

Monthly Planner

MONTH OF:

MONDAY	TUESDAY	WEDNESDAY	THURSDAY

Monthly Planner

MONTH OF:

FRIDAY	SATURDAY	SUNDAY	NOTES

Monthly Planner

MONTH OF:

MONDAY	TUESDAY	WEDNESDAY	THURSDAY

Monthly Planner

FRIDAY	SATURDAY	SUNDAY	NOTES

Monthly Planner

MONTH OF:

MONDAY	TUESDAY	WEDNESDAY	THURSDAY

Monthly Planner

FRIDAY	SATURDAY	SUNDAY	NOTES

Monthly Planner

MONTH OF:

MONDAY	TUESDAY	WEDNESDAY	THURSDAY

Monthly Planner

MONTH OF:

FRIDAY	SATURDAY	SUNDAY	NOTES

Monthly Planner

MONTH OF:

MONDAY	TUESDAY	WEDNESDAY	THURSDAY

Monthly Planner

FRIDAY	SATURDAY	SUNDAY	NOTES

Monthly Planner

MONTH OF:

MONDAY	TUESDAY	WEDNESDAY	THURSDAY

Monthly Planner

FRIDAY	SATURDAY	SUNDAY	NOTES

Monthly Planner

MONTH OF:

MONDAY	TUESDAY	WEDNESDAY	THURSDAY

Monthly Planner

MONTH OF:

FRIDAY	SATURDAY	SUNDAY	NOTES

Monthly Planner

MONTH OF:

MONDAY	TUESDAY	WEDNESDAY	THURSDAY

Monthly Planner

FRIDAY	SATURDAY	SUNDAY	NOTES

Monthly Planner

MONDAY	TUESDAY	WEDNESDAY	THURSDAY

Monthly Planner

FRIDAY	SATURDAY	SUNDAY	NOTES

Monthly Planner

MONTH OF:

MONDAY	TUESDAY	WEDNESDAY	THURSDAY

Monthly Planner

MONTH OF:

FRIDAY	SATURDAY	SUNDAY	NOTES

Monthly Planner

MONDAY	TUESDAY	WEDNESDAY	THURSDAY

Monthly Planner

FRIDAY	SATURDAY	SUNDAY	NOTES

Equipment List

ITEM	DESCRIPTION	PURCHASE DATE	PURCHASE AMOUNT

Props Inventory

ITEMS & DESCRIPTION	STYLE

Mileage Tracker

<table>
<tr><th rowspan="2">DATE</th><th rowspan="2">REASON</th><th colspan="2">ODOMETER</th><th rowspan="2">TOTAL
MILEAGE</th></tr>
<tr><th>START</th><th>END</th></tr>
</table>

Income Tracker

DATE	ORDER NO.	CASH/ CARD	DESCRIPTION	PURCHASE AMOUNT

Income Tracker

DATE	ORDER NO.	CASH/ CARD	DESCRIPTION	PURCHASE AMOUNT

Expense Tracker

DATE	DESCRIPTION	AMOUNT

Expense Tracker

DATE	DESCRIPTION	AMOUNT

Locations List

LOCATION	DESCRIPTION	ENTRY FEE	OPENING TIME	RATING
				◇◇◇◇◇
				◇◇◇◇◇
				◇◇◇◇◇
				◇◇◇◇◇
				◇◇◇◇◇
				◇◇◇◇◇
				◇◇◇◇◇
				◇◇◇◇◇
				◇◇◇◇◇
				◇◇◇◇◇
				◇◇◇◇◇
				◇◇◇◇◇
				◇◇◇◇◇

Photo Session Ideas

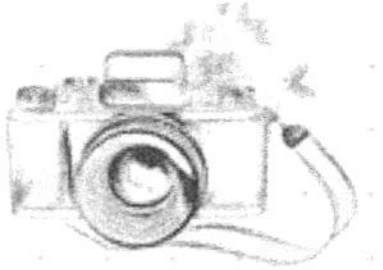

Photo Session Ideas

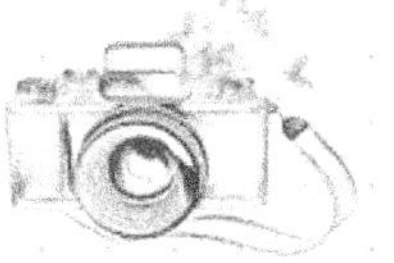

Photo Session Ideas

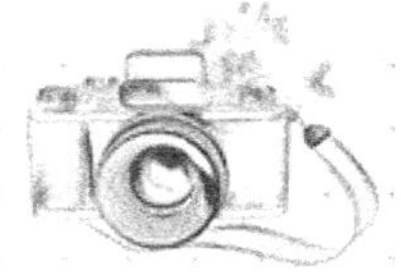

Photo Session Ideas

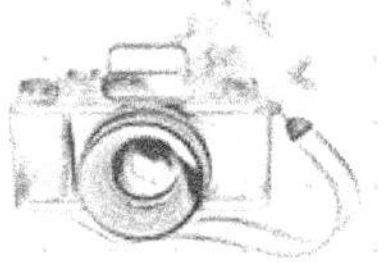

Photo Session Ideas

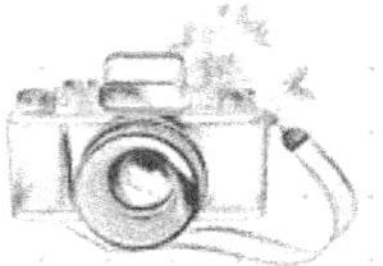

Photo Session Ideas

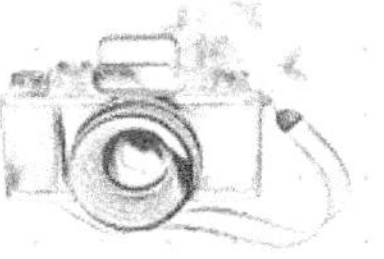

Photo Session Ideas

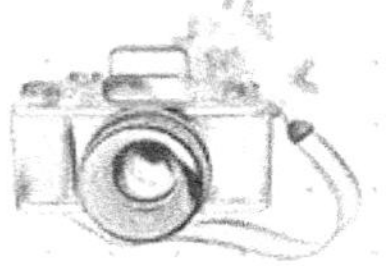

Photo Session Ideas

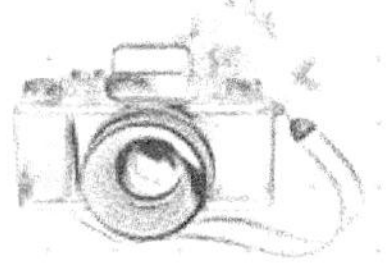

Photo Session Ideas

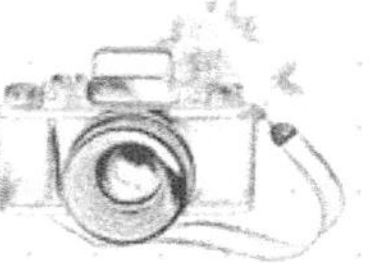

Photo Session Ideas

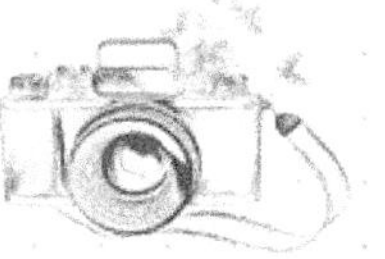

Mini Sessions

EVENT TITLE:

DATE: LOCATION:

THEME: PRICE:

INCLUSIONS: PROPS:

CLIENT SCHEDULE:

CLIENT   PHONE/EMAIL   TIME   PAID?

TOTAL:

Mini Sessions

EVENT TITLE:

DATE: LOCATION:

THEME: PRICE:

INCLUSIONS: PROPS:

CLIENT SCHEDULE:

CLIENT	PHONE/EMAIL	TIME	PAID?

TOTAL:

Mini Sessions

EVENT TITLE:

DATE: LOCATION:

THEME: PRICE:

INCLUSIONS: PROPS:

CLIENT SCHEDULE:

CLIENT	PHONE/EMAIL	TIME	PAID?

TOTAL:

Mini Sessions

EVENT TITLE:

DATE: LOCATION:

THEME: PRICE:

INCLUSIONS: PROPS:

CLIENT SCHEDULE:

CLIENT	PHONE/EMAIL	TIME	PAID?

TOTAL:

Mini Sessions

EVENT TITLE:

DATE: LOCATION:

THEME: PRICE:

INCLUSIONS: PROPS:

CLIENT SCHEDULE:

CLIENT	PHONE/EMAIL	TIME	PAID?

TOTAL:

Mini Sessions

EVENT TITLE:

DATE: LOCATION:

THEME: PRICE:

INCLUSIONS: PROPS:

CLIENT SCHEDULE:

CLIENT	PHONE/EMAIL	TIME	PAID?

TOTAL:

Mini Sessions

EVENT TITLE:

DATE: LOCATION:

THEME: PRICE:

INCLUSIONS: PROPS:

CLIENT SCHEDULE:

CLIENT   PHONE/EMAIL   TIME   PAID?

TOTAL:

Mini Sessions

EVENT TITLE:

DATE: LOCATION:

THEME: PRICE:

INCLUSIONS: PROPS:

CLIENT SCHEDULE:

CLIENT	PHONE/EMAIL	TIME	PAID?

TOTAL:

Mini Sessions

EVENT TITLE:

DATE: LOCATION:

THEME: PRICE:

INCLUSIONS: PROPS:

CLIENT SCHEDULE:

CLIENT   PHONE/EMAIL   TIME   PAID?

TOTAL:

Mini Sessions

EVENT TITLE:

DATE: LOCATION:

THEME: PRICE:

INCLUSIONS: PROPS:

CLIENT SCHEDULE:

CLIENT	PHONE/EMAIL	TIME	PAID?

TOTAL:

Photo Session Planner

CLIENT

ORDER NO.

EMAIL

FULL PRICE

PHONE

DEPOSIT

DATE/TIME

BALANCE DUE

LOCATION

TRAVEL TIME

PHOTO SHOOT TYPE

IMPORTANT SHOTS

ADDITIONAL INFO

READINESS CHECKLIST:

Contract Signed

Reminders Sent

Get Location Permit

Check Camera (Clean Lens)

Charge Battery

Check Cards

Extra Cards/Batteries

Tripod

Pack All Equipment

Check Map/Satnav

Pack Snacks/Water

PHOTO SESSION DETAILS/IDEAS

Client Workflow

Photo Session Planner

CLIENT

EMAIL

PHONE

DATE/TIME

LOCATION

TRAVEL TIME

PHOTO SHOOT TYPE

IMPORTANT SHOTS

ADDITIONAL INFO

PHOTO SESSION DETAILS/IDEAS

ORDER NO.

FULL PRICE

DEPOSIT

BALANCE DUE

READINESS CHECKLIST:

Contract Signed

Reminders Sent

Get Location Permit

Check Camera (Clean Lens)

Charge Battery

Check Cards

Extra Cards/Batteries

Tripod

Pack All Equipment

Check Map/Satnav

Pack Snacks/Water

Client Workflow

Photo Session Planner

CLIENT

EMAIL

PHONE

DATE/TIME

LOCATION

TRAVEL TIME

PHOTO SHOOT TYPE

IMPORTANT SHOTS

ADDITIONAL INFO

PHOTO SESSION DETAILS/IDEAS

ORDER NO.
FULL PRICE
DEPOSIT
BALANCE DUE

READINESS CHECKLIST:

- Contract Signed
- Reminders Sent
- Get Location Permit
- Check Camera (Clean Lens)
- Charge Battery
- Check Cards
- Extra Cards/Batteries
- Tripod
- Pack All Equipment
- Check Map/Satnav
- Pack Snacks/Water

Client Workflow

Photo Session Planner

CLIENT

EMAIL

PHONE

DATE/TIME

LOCATION

TRAVEL TIME

PHOTO SHOOT TYPE

IMPORTANT SHOTS

ADDITIONAL INFO

PHOTO SESSION DETAILS/IDEAS

ORDER NO.

FULL PRICE

DEPOSIT

BALANCE DUE

READINESS CHECKLIST:

Contract Signed

Reminders Sent

Get Location Permit

Check Camera (Clean Lens)

Charge Battery

Check Cards

Extra Cards/Batteries

Tripod

Pack All Equipment

Check Map/Satnav

Pack Snacks/Water

Client Workflow

Photo Session Planner

CLIENT

EMAIL

PHONE

DATE/TIME

LOCATION

TRAVEL TIME

PHOTO SHOOT TYPE

IMPORTANT SHOTS

ADDITIONAL INFO

PHOTO SESSION DETAILS/IDEAS

| ORDER NO. |
| FULL PRICE |
| DEPOSIT |
| BALANCE DUE |

READINESS CHECKLIST:

- Contract Signed
- Reminders Sent
- Get Location Permit
- Check Camera (Clean Lens)
- Charge Battery
- Check Cards
- Extra Cards/Batteries
- Tripod
- Pack All Equipment
- Check Map/Satnav
- Pack Snacks/Water

Client Workflow

Photo Session Planner

CLIENT

EMAIL

PHONE

DATE/TIME

LOCATION

TRAVEL TIME

PHOTO SHOOT TYPE

IMPORTANT SHOTS

ADDITIONAL INFO

PHOTO SESSION DETAILS/IDEAS

ORDER NO.

FULL PRICE

DEPOSIT

BALANCE DUE

READINESS CHECKLIST:

- Contract Signed
- Reminders Sent
- Get Location Permit
- Check Camera (Clean Lens)
- Charge Battery
- Check Cards
- Extra Cards/Batteries
- Tripod
- Pack All Equipment
- Check Map/Satnav
- Pack Snacks/Water

Client Workflow

Photo Session Planner

CLIENT

EMAIL

PHONE

DATE/TIME

LOCATION

TRAVEL TIME

PHOTO SHOOT TYPE

IMPORTANT SHOTS

ADDITIONAL INFO

PHOTO SESSION DETAILS/IDEAS

ORDER NO.

FULL PRICE

DEPOSIT

BALANCE DUE

READINESS CHECKLIST:

Contract Signed

Reminders Sent

Get Location Permit

Check Camera (Clean Lens)

Charge Battery

Check Cards

Extra Cards/Batteries

Tripod

Pack All Equipment

Check Map/Satnav

Pack Snacks/Water

Client Workflow

Photo Session Planner

CLIENT

EMAIL

PHONE

DATE/TIME

LOCATION

TRAVEL TIME

PHOTO SHOOT TYPE

IMPORTANT SHOTS

ADDITIONAL INFO

PHOTO SESSION DETAILS/IDEAS

| ORDER NO. |
| FULL PRICE |
| DEPOSIT |
| BALANCE DUE |

READINESS CHECKLIST:

- Contract Signed
- Reminders Sent
- Get Location Permit
- Check Camera (Clean Lens)
- Charge Battery
- Check Cards
- Extra Cards/Batteries
- Tripod
- Pack All Equipment
- Check Map/Satnav
- Pack Snacks/Water

Client Workflow

Photo Session Planner

CLIENT

EMAIL

PHONE

DATE/TIME

LOCATION

TRAVEL TIME

PHOTO SHOOT TYPE

IMPORTANT SHOTS

ADDITIONAL INFO

PHOTO SESSION DETAILS/IDEAS

ORDER NO.

FULL PRICE

DEPOSIT

BALANCE DUE

READINESS CHECKLIST:

Contract Signed

Reminders Sent

Get Location Permit

Check Camera (Clean Lens)

Charge Battery

Check Cards

Extra Cards/Batteries

Tripod

Pack All Equipment

Check Map/Satnav

Pack Snacks/Water

Client Workflow

Photo Session Planner

CLIENT

EMAIL

PHONE

DATE/TIME

LOCATION

TRAVEL TIME

PHOTO SHOOT TYPE

ORDER NO.

FULL PRICE

DEPOSIT

BALANCE DUE

IMPORTANT SHOTS

ADDITIONAL INFO

PHOTO SESSION DETAILS/IDEAS

READINESS CHECKLIST:

- Contract Signed
- Reminders Sent
- Get Location Permit
- Check Camera (Clean Lens)
- Charge Battery
- Check Cards
- Extra Cards/Batteries
- Tripod
- Pack All Equipment
- Check Map/Satnav
- Pack Snacks/Water

Client Workflow

Photo Session Planner

CLIENT

ORDER NO.

EMAIL

FULL PRICE

PHONE

DEPOSIT

DATE/TIME

LOCATION

BALANCE DUE

TRAVEL TIME

PHOTO SHOOT TYPE

IMPORTANT SHOTS

ADDITIONAL INFO

PHOTO SESSION DETAILS/IDEAS

READINESS CHECKLIST:

- Contract Signed
- Reminders Sent
- Get Location Permit
- Check Camera (Clean Lens)
- Charge Battery
- Check Cards
- Extra Cards/Batteries
- Tripod
- Pack All Equipment
- Check Map/Satnav
- Pack Snacks/Water

Client Workflow

Photo Session Planner

CLIENT

EMAIL

PHONE

DATE/TIME

LOCATION

TRAVEL TIME

PHOTO SHOOT TYPE

IMPORTANT SHOTS

ADDITIONAL INFO

PHOTO SESSION DETAILS/IDEAS

ORDER NO.

FULL PRICE

DEPOSIT

BALANCE DUE

READINESS CHECKLIST:

- Contract Signed
- Reminders Sent
- Get Location Permit
- Check Camera (Clean Lens)
- Charge Battery
- Check Cards
- Extra Cards/Batteries
- Tripod
- Pack All Equipment
- Check Map/Satnav
- Pack Snacks/Water

Client Workflow

Photo Session Planner

CLIENT

EMAIL

PHONE

DATE/TIME

LOCATION

TRAVEL TIME

PHOTO SHOOT TYPE

IMPORTANT SHOTS

ADDITIONAL INFO

PHOTO SESSION DETAILS/IDEAS

| ORDER NO. |
| FULL PRICE |
| DEPOSIT |
| BALANCE DUE |

READINESS CHECKLIST:

Contract Signed

Reminders Sent

Get Location Permit

Check Camera (Clean Lens)

Charge Battery

Check Cards

Extra Cards/Batteries

Tripod

Pack All Equipment

Check Map/Satnav

Pack Snacks/Water

Client Workflow

Photo Session Planner

CLIENT

EMAIL

PHONE

DATE/TIME

LOCATION

TRAVEL TIME

PHOTO SHOOT TYPE

IMPORTANT SHOTS

ADDITIONAL INFO

PHOTO SESSION DETAILS/IDEAS

| ORDER NO. |
| FULL PRICE |
| DEPOSIT |
| BALANCE DUE |

READINESS CHECKLIST:

Contract Signed

Reminders Sent

Get Location Permit

Check Camera (Clean Lens)

Charge Battery

Check Cards

Extra Cards/Batteries

Tripod

Pack All Equipment

Check Map/Satnav

Pack Snacks/Water

Client Workflow

Photo Session Planner

CLIENT

EMAIL

PHONE

DATE/TIME

LOCATION

TRAVEL TIME

PHOTO SHOOT TYPE

IMPORTANT SHOTS

ADDITIONAL INFO

PHOTO SESSION DETAILS/IDEAS

ORDER NO.

FULL PRICE

DEPOSIT

BALANCE DUE

READINESS CHECKLIST:

- Contract Signed
- Reminders Sent
- Get Location Permit
- Check Camera (Clean Lens)
- Charge Battery
- Check Cards
- Extra Cards/Batteries
- Tripod
- Pack All Equipment
- Check Map/Satnav
- Pack Snacks/Water

Client Workflow

Photo Session Planner

CLIENT

EMAIL

PHONE

DATE/TIME

LOCATION

TRAVEL TIME

PHOTO SHOOT TYPE

IMPORTANT SHOTS

ADDITIONAL INFO

PHOTO SESSION DETAILS/IDEAS

ORDER NO.

FULL PRICE

DEPOSIT

BALANCE DUE

READINESS CHECKLIST:

Contract Signed

Reminders Sent

Get Location Permit

Check Camera (Clean Lens)

Charge Battery

Check Cards

Extra Cards/Batteries

Tripod

Pack All Equipment

Check Map/Satnav

Pack Snacks/Water

Client Workflow

Photo Session Planner

CLIENT

EMAIL

PHONE

DATE/TIME

LOCATION

TRAVEL TIME

PHOTO SHOOT TYPE

IMPORTANT SHOTS

ADDITIONAL INFO

PHOTO SESSION DETAILS/IDEAS

| ORDER NO. |
| FULL PRICE |
| DEPOSIT |
| BALANCE DUE |

READINESS CHECKLIST:

Contract Signed

Reminders Sent

Get Location Permit

Check Camera (Clean Lens)

Charge Battery

Check Cards

Extra Cards/Batteries

Tripod

Pack All Equipment

Check Map/Satnav

Pack Snacks/Water

Client Workflow

Photo Session Planner

CLIENT

EMAIL

PHONE

DATE/TIME

LOCATION

TRAVEL TIME

PHOTO SHOOT TYPE

IMPORTANT SHOTS

ADDITIONAL INFO

PHOTO SESSION DETAILS/IDEAS

ORDER NO.

FULL PRICE

DEPOSIT

BALANCE DUE

READINESS CHECKLIST:

Contract Signed

Reminders Sent

Get Location Permit

Check Camera (Clean Lens)

Charge Battery

Check Cards

Extra Cards/Batteries

Tripod

Pack All Equipment

Check Map/Satnav

Pack Snacks/Water

Client Workflow

Photo Session Planner

CLIENT

EMAIL

PHONE

DATE/TIME

LOCATION

TRAVEL TIME

PHOTO SHOOT TYPE

IMPORTANT SHOTS

ADDITIONAL INFO

PHOTO SESSION DETAILS/IDEAS

| ORDER NO. |
| FULL PRICE |
| DEPOSIT |
| BALANCE DUE |

READINESS CHECKLIST:

Contract Signed

Reminders Sent

Get Location Permit

Check Camera (Clean Lens)

Charge Battery

Check Cards

Extra Cards/Batteries

Tripod

Pack All Equipment

Check Map/Satnav

Pack Snacks/Water

Client Workflow

Photo Session Planner

CLIENT

EMAIL

PHONE

DATE/TIME

LOCATION

TRAVEL TIME

PHOTO SHOOT TYPE

IMPORTANT SHOTS

ADDITIONAL INFO

PHOTO SESSION DETAILS/IDEAS

ORDER NO.

FULL PRICE

DEPOSIT

BALANCE DUE

READINESS CHECKLIST:

- Contract Signed
- Reminders Sent
- Get Location Permit
- Check Camera (Clean Lens)
- Charge Battery
- Check Cards
- Extra Cards/Batteries
- Tripod
- Pack All Equipment
- Check Map/Satnav
- Pack Snacks/Water

Client Workflow

Photo Session Planner

CLIENT

EMAIL

PHONE

DATE/TIME

LOCATION

TRAVEL TIME

PHOTO SHOOT TYPE

IMPORTANT SHOTS

ADDITIONAL INFO

PHOTO SESSION DETAILS/IDEAS

| ORDER NO. |
| FULL PRICE |
| DEPOSIT |
| BALANCE DUE |

READINESS CHECKLIST:

Contract Signed

Reminders Sent

Get Location Permit

Check Camera (Clean Lens)

Charge Battery

Check Cards

Extra Cards/Batteries

Tripod

Pack All Equipment

Check Map/Satnav

Pack Snacks/Water

Client Workflow

Photo Session Planner

CLIENT

EMAIL

PHONE

DATE/TIME

LOCATION

TRAVEL TIME

PHOTO SHOOT TYPE

IMPORTANT SHOTS

ADDITIONAL INFO

PHOTO SESSION DETAILS/IDEAS

| ORDER NO. |
| FULL PRICE |
| DEPOSIT |
| BALANCE DUE |

READINESS CHECKLIST:

Contract Signed

Reminders Sent

Get Location Permit

Check Camera (Clean Lens)

Charge Battery

Check Cards

Extra Cards/Batteries

Tripod

Pack All Equipment

Check Map/Satnav

Pack Snacks/Water

Client Workflow

Photo Session Planner

CLIENT

EMAIL

PHONE

DATE/TIME

LOCATION

TRAVEL TIME

PHOTO SHOOT TYPE

IMPORTANT SHOTS

ADDITIONAL INFO

PHOTO SESSION DETAILS/IDEAS

ORDER NO.

FULL PRICE

DEPOSIT

BALANCE DUE

READINESS CHECKLIST:

Contract Signed

Reminders Sent

Get Location Permit

Check Camera (Clean Lens)

Charge Battery

Check Cards

Extra Cards/Batteries

Tripod

Pack All Equipment

Check Map/Satnav

Pack Snacks/Water

Client Workflow

Photo Session Planner

CLIENT

EMAIL

PHONE

DATE/TIME

LOCATION

TRAVEL TIME

PHOTO SHOOT TYPE

IMPORTANT SHOTS

ADDITIONAL INFO

PHOTO SESSION DETAILS/IDEAS

ORDER NO.

FULL PRICE

DEPOSIT

BALANCE DUE

READINESS CHECKLIST:

- Contract Signed
- Reminders Sent
- Get Location Permit
- Check Camera (Clean Lens)
- Charge Battery
- Check Cards
- Extra Cards/Batteries
- Tripod
- Pack All Equipment
- Check Map/Satnav
- Pack Snacks/Water

Client Workflow

Photo Session Planner

CLIENT

| ORDER NO. |
| FULL PRICE |
| DEPOSIT |
| BALANCE DUE |

EMAIL

PHONE

DATE/TIME

LOCATION

TRAVEL TIME

PHOTO SHOOT TYPE

IMPORTANT SHOTS

ADDITIONAL INFO

PHOTO SESSION DETAILS/IDEAS

READINESS CHECKLIST:

- Contract Signed
- Reminders Sent
- Get Location Permit
- Check Camera (Clean Lens)
- Charge Battery
- Check Cards
- Extra Cards/Batteries
- Tripod
- Pack All Equipment
- Check Map/Satnav
- Pack Snacks/Water

Client Workflow

Photo Session Planner

CLIENT

EMAIL

PHONE

DATE/TIME

LOCATION

TRAVEL TIME

PHOTO SHOOT TYPE

IMPORTANT SHOTS

ADDITIONAL INFO

PHOTO SESSION DETAILS/IDEAS

ORDER NO.

FULL PRICE

DEPOSIT

BALANCE DUE

READINESS CHECKLIST:

Contract Signed

Reminders Sent

Get Location Permit

Check Camera (Clean Lens)

Charge Battery

Check Cards

Extra Cards/Batteries

Tripod

Pack All Equipment

Check Map/Satnav

Pack Snacks/Water

Client Workflow

Photo Session Planner

CLIENT

EMAIL

PHONE

DATE/TIME

LOCATION

TRAVEL TIME

PHOTO SHOOT TYPE

IMPORTANT SHOTS

ADDITIONAL INFO

PHOTO SESSION DETAILS/IDEAS

ORDER NO.
FULL PRICE
DEPOSIT
BALANCE DUE

READINESS CHECKLIST:

Contract Signed

Reminders Sent

Get Location Permit

Check Camera (Clean Lens)

Charge Battery

Check Cards

Extra Cards/Batteries

Tripod

Pack All Equipment

Check Map/Satnav

Pack Snacks/Water

Client Workflow

Photo Session Planner

CLIENT

EMAIL

PHONE

DATE/TIME

LOCATION

TRAVEL TIME

PHOTO SHOOT TYPE

IMPORTANT SHOTS

ADDITIONAL INFO

PHOTO SESSION DETAILS/IDEAS

| ORDER NO. |
| FULL PRICE |
| DEPOSIT |
| BALANCE DUE |

READINESS CHECKLIST:

Contract Signed

Reminders Sent

Get Location Permit

Check Camera (Clean Lens)

Charge Battery

Check Cards

Extra Cards/Batteries

Tripod

Pack All Equipment

Check Map/Satnav

Pack Snacks/Water

Client Workflow

Photo Session Planner

CLIENT

EMAIL

PHONE

DATE/TIME

LOCATION

TRAVEL TIME

PHOTO SHOOT TYPE

IMPORTANT SHOTS

ADDITIONAL INFO

PHOTO SESSION DETAILS/IDEAS

| ORDER NO. |
| FULL PRICE |
| DEPOSIT |
| BALANCE DUE |

READINESS CHECKLIST:

Contract Signed

Reminders Sent

Get Location Permit

Check Camera (Clean Lens)

Charge Battery

Check Cards

Extra Cards/Batteries

Tripod

Pack All Equipment

Check Map/Satnav

Pack Snacks/Water

Client Workflow

Photo Session Planner

CLIENT

EMAIL

PHONE

DATE/TIME

LOCATION

TRAVEL TIME

PHOTO SHOOT TYPE

IMPORTANT SHOTS

ADDITIONAL INFO

PHOTO SESSION DETAILS/IDEAS

| ORDER NO. |
| FULL PRICE |
| DEPOSIT |
| BALANCE DUE |

READINESS CHECKLIST:

Contract Signed

Reminders Sent

Get Location Permit

Check Camera (Clean Lens)

Charge Battery

Check Cards

Extra Cards/Batteries

Tripod

Pack All Equipment

Check Map/Satnav

Pack Snacks/Water

Client Workflow

Photo Session Planner

CLIENT

ORDER NO.

EMAIL

FULL PRICE

PHONE

DEPOSIT

DATE/TIME

BALANCE DUE

LOCATION

TRAVEL TIME

PHOTO SHOOT TYPE

IMPORTANT SHOTS

ADDITIONAL INFO

PHOTO SESSION DETAILS/IDEAS

READINESS CHECKLIST:

- Contract Signed
- Reminders Sent
- Get Location Permit
- Check Camera (Clean Lens)
- Charge Battery
- Check Cards
- Extra Cards/Batteries
- Tripod
- Pack All Equipment
- Check Map/Satnav
- Pack Snacks/Water

Client Workflow

Photo Session Planner

CLIENT

EMAIL

PHONE

DATE/TIME

LOCATION

TRAVEL TIME

PHOTO SHOOT TYPE

IMPORTANT SHOTS

ADDITIONAL INFO

PHOTO SESSION DETAILS/IDEAS

ORDER NO.

FULL PRICE

DEPOSIT

BALANCE DUE

READINESS CHECKLIST:

- Contract Signed
- Reminders Sent
- Get Location Permit
- Check Camera (Clean Lens)
- Charge Battery
- Check Cards
- Extra Cards/Batteries
- Tripod
- Pack All Equipment
- Check Map/Satnav
- Pack Snacks/Water

Client Workflow

Photo Session Planner

CLIENT

EMAIL

PHONE

DATE/TIME

LOCATION

TRAVEL TIME

PHOTO SHOOT TYPE

IMPORTANT SHOTS

ADDITIONAL INFO

PHOTO SESSION DETAILS/IDEAS

| ORDER NO. |
| FULL PRICE |
| DEPOSIT |
| BALANCE DUE |

READINESS CHECKLIST:

Contract Signed

Reminders Sent

Get Location Permit

Check Camera (Clean Lens)

Charge Battery

Check Cards

Extra Cards/Batteries

Tripod

Pack All Equipment

Check Map/Satnav

Pack Snacks/Water

Client Workflow

Photo Session Planner

CLIENT

EMAIL

PHONE

DATE/TIME

LOCATION

TRAVEL TIME

PHOTO SHOOT TYPE

IMPORTANT SHOTS

ADDITIONAL INFO

PHOTO SESSION DETAILS/IDEAS

ORDER NO.

FULL PRICE

DEPOSIT

BALANCE DUE

READINESS CHECKLIST:

Contract Signed

Reminders Sent

Get Location Permit

Check Camera (Clean Lens)

Charge Battery

Check Cards

Extra Cards/Batteries

Tripod

Pack All Equipment

Check Map/Satnav

Pack Snacks/Water

Client Workflow

Photo Session Planner

CLIENT

EMAIL

PHONE

DATE/TIME

LOCATION

TRAVEL TIME

PHOTO SHOOT TYPE

IMPORTANT SHOTS

ADDITIONAL INFO

PHOTO SESSION DETAILS/IDEAS

ORDER NO.

FULL PRICE

DEPOSIT

BALANCE DUE

READINESS CHECKLIST:

- Contract Signed
- Reminders Sent
- Get Location Permit
- Check Camera (Clean Lens)
- Charge Battery
- Check Cards
- Extra Cards/Batteries
- Tripod
- Pack All Equipment
- Check Map/Satnav
- Pack Snacks/Water

Client Workflow